Six Steps

—— *to* ——

Reduce Stress

GREGORY L. JANTZ, PHD
WITH ANN MCMURRAY

AspirePress

Carson, California

AspirePress

Six Steps to Reduce Stress
Copyright © 2016 Gregory L. Jantz
All rights reserved.
Aspire Press, an imprint of Rose Publishing, Inc.
17909 Adria Maru Lane
Carson, CA 90746 USA
www.aspirepress.com

Register your book at www.rose-publishing.com/register
and receive a FREE *How to Study the Bible* PDF
to print for your personal or ministry use.

The views and opinions expressed in this book are those of the author(s) and do not necessarily express the views of Aspire Press, nor is this book intended to be a substitute for mental health treatment or professional counseling.

Printed in the United States of America
021016RRD

Contents

The Stress-Full Life

It's 3:23 a.m. and you're suddenly awake. You're not sure what's awoken you, because the room is eerily quiet. Nothing appears wrong in the near dark, but you're suddenly and completely awake. Whatever you were dreaming about is gone, replaced by a vague sense of alarm. Your body is aching to go back to sleep, but your mind has switched into full-blown stress mode.

Your thoughts are racing, as you think about all the things you haven't done. You try to force yourself back to sleep, because you know you'll pay the price tomorrow. So much to do, so little time, and, now, so little sleep! How will you ever get it all done? It's 3:23 a.m. and you're already behind for the day.

The numbers on the alarm clock mock you as you lay awake and watch the night slip away. Now you're not only thinking about the things you've got to do, you're also reliving the things you've done—that conflict with your coworker, the tense conversation with your teen, the mistake you made at work.

All is quiet in your bedroom, but your mind is in bedlam. Every barely concealed fear and anxiety has a feeding frenzy on all those should-haves and what-ifs and must-dos that pop up in the middle of your night. The pressure to do it all, find it all, and fix it all feels like a crushing weight. You feel pressure not only to get it all done but to do it all well, because if you don't, disaster awaits. And then what will you do? How will you cope? With all of this stress, how is anyone supposed to get a good night's sleep?

■ ■ ■

If you feel stressed out, you are not alone. According to a recent report by the American Psychological Association (APA), "75 percent of Americans report experiencing at least one symptom of stress in the past month."[1] In 2014, the number of adults in the United States, per the US Census Bureau, was around 242 million.[2] If you're feeling stressed, this means you've joined almost 182 million Americans this month who feel the same way.

Does that number surprise you? Are you surprised that three-fourths of the adults in this country struggle with stress at some level? You probably aren't surprised, if you've admitted your own stress to others. News sites are full of stories about our stress. But what are we stressing about? According to the APA report:

- A majority of us are stressed out about money (64 percent).

- Many of us feel stressed about our jobs (60 percent).

- Almost half of us are stressed about the economy in general (49 percent).

- We are also stressed about family responsibilities (47 percent).

- And we experience stress over personal health concerns (46 percent).

We're stressed out, and that negatively affects our health, which contributes to even more stress. This spiral is not headed in a good direction.

What does stress do to us?

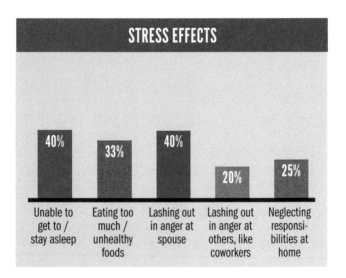

How do we commonly show our stress?

- Overall, anger or irritability tops the list of stress symptoms (37 percent).

- Nervousness/anxiousness is a close second (35 percent).

- Lack of interest/motivation comes in next (34 percent).

- And the final three most common symptoms are fatigue, feeling overwhelmed, and feeling depressed/sad (each at 32 percent).

Does that sound like you? Angry yet apathetic; anxious yet depressed; keyed-up yet tired; overwhelmed and sad. Each of us has probably felt this way at times, but what do you do if "at times" is becoming all the time?

What role does faith play in stress? A recent Pew Research Center *Religion and Public Life* report found almost 71 percent of American adults identify as Christian.[3] If 71 percent of adult Americans identify as Christians and if 75 percent of all adult Americans identify with stress, then Christians are not immune from stress. How can this happen to people who claim to follow the words of Jesus: "Can any one of you by worrying add a single hour to your life?" (Matthew 6:27).

The dictionary defines stress using a variety of images: mental tension, worry,

> In times of stress, turn to God for comfort.
>
> "AS PRESSURE AND STRESS BEAR DOWN ON ME, I FIND JOY IN YOUR COMMANDS."
> —PSALM 119:143, NLT

anxiety, strain, and/or pressure. If you Google images of stress, you're confronted with pictures of unhappy, overwhelmed people, ready to explode. How did life become so stressful? How can we break out of the stress vice of our culture and find peace? Like the frog slowly boiling in the pot, we need to realize the water's getting hotter and the time has come to jump out.

Living *Under* Red Alert

A body under stress is a body living under Red Alert. Stress hormones surge through the blood stream, activating bodily systems such as heart rate, blood pressure, muscle tension, respiration, and digestion. The head pounds, the heart races, the jaw clenches, hands shake, and pores sweat.

If you need to swerve to avoid an oncoming car or race to an injured child, this state of Red Alert is useful, as your body is prepared to move in maximum and extreme ways to deal with danger. Stress, however, creates a sense of false danger and keeps your body ramped up to Red Alert where and when no immediate danger exists.

A BODY UNDER STRESS IS A BODY LIVING UNDER RED ALERT.

Chronic stress puts a tremendous strain on you physically and psychologically. Constant waves of adrenaline (also called epinephrine) and cortisol (also called hydrocortisone) supercharge your systems, burning up resources and leaving you shaky and depleted.

Signs *of* Stress

The symptoms of stress can show up in unexpected ways. You probably can relate to the most common stress symptoms reported by other American adults (discussed earlier), but consider the following questions and whether you're experiencing any of the following signs of a stress-filled life:

☐ WHAT IS YOUR CURRENT RESTING HEART RATE?

Stress leaves you energized and may cause you to have difficulty relaxing, so your heart may have difficulty returning to a low resting rate.

☐ WHAT IS YOUR RESTING BLOOD PRESSURE?

The more stressed you are, the harder your cardiovascular system works. This can create a situation where your blood pressure spikes and then takes longer than normal to fall back down to within a normal range.

☐ DO YOU FIND YOURSELF HYPERVENTILATING?

Deep breathing in the face of physical exertion is useful, as it allows for increased oxygen to be used by the body. Hyperventilation, or overbreathing, however, creates a situation where the body releases too much carbon dioxide, resulting in dizziness, tingling, headache, and general weakness.

☐ HAS YOUR DENTIST MENTIONED THAT YOU GRIND YOUR TEETH AT NIGHT?

Teeth grinding is a known symptom of stress, as clenching of the jaw muscles causes the teeth to work against each other, even during sleep.

☐ DO YOU FIND YOURSELF BREAKING OUT IN PIMPLES, ACNE, OR SKIN RASHES?

Stress produces toxins in the body that can be excreted through the largest organ you have— your skin.

☐ ARE YOU ALWAYS QUICK TO CATCH WHATEVER COLD OR FLU SEEMS TO BE GOING AROUND?

Stress puts a tremendous strain on your immune system, which can result in lower resistance to illnesses and infections.

☐ IS YOUR INTEREST IN OR ABILITY TO HAVE SEX FLAGGING?

Stress can suck all the sexual energy out of a room, leaving you tired, unmotivated, and uninterested. Stress can also lead to painful periods in women and episodes of impotence in men.

☐ ARE YOU GAINING WEIGHT, OR HAVE YOU LOST INTEREST IN FOOD?

Food is a common way people cope with stress—either by self-medicating through food or losing their appetites. Large shifts in weight—either up or down—can indicate the presence of stress.

☐ ARE YOU EATING NORMALLY AND EASILY DIGESTING WHAT YOU EAT?

In response to stress, some people may eat too much, too little, or the wrong types of foods. In addition, the physical effects of stress can interfere with the process of digestion and elimination.

☐ DO YOU FIND YOURSELF RANTING OR VENTING YOUR FEELINGS OF ANGER?

An emotional rant or venting may make you feel more relaxed, more relieved, because stress can be painful, and people in pain may react strongly in anger. Anger is a powerful physical and psychological response that can bleed off some of the effects of stress.

☐ DO YOU FIND YOURSELF REPEATEDLY USING OVER-THE-COUNTER SLEEP AIDS OR ANTIHISTAMINES?

What about prescribed medications, such as anti-anxiety medications? Overuse of such drugs may be a sign that the problem is stress, and these pharmaceuticals do not offer long-term solutions to the problem.

☐ DO YOU PICK AT SCABS OR PULL YOUR HAIR? DO YOU BITE YOUR NAILS OR CHEW YOUR CUTICLES?

Such small, repetitive habits can be a sign of a large stress problem.

☐ DO YOU TURN TO ALCOHOL MORE AND MORE OFTEN IN ORDER TO RELAX?

Alcohol is a powerful depressant that some may use or abuse to depress an overactive central nervous system ramped up by stress.

☐ DO YOU REACH FOR A CIGARETTE IN ORDER TO RELAX?

Nicotine can act as both a depressant and a stimulant, allowing you to feel relaxed and energized at the same time.

☐ DO YOU FIND YOURSELF POPPING OVER-THE-COUNTER ANALGESICS (SUCH AS ASPIRIN, ACETAMINOPHEN, OR IBUPROFEN) LIKE THEY WERE CANDY?

Stress, and often the increase in blood pressure associated with stress, can cause headaches—sometimes even severe ones or even migraines.

☐ DO YOU EXPERIENCE MUSCLE FATIGUE OR PAIN THAT DOESN'T SEEM TO GO AWAY?

One of the effects of stress is muscle tension, and some people tend to hold their stress in certain parts of their bodies, such as shoulders, neck, or back.

As a busy professional, husband, and father, I feel the effects of stress in my own life. As a therapist, I often see the effects of stress in the lives of those I work with on a regular basis. For some people, these stress effects are so familiar, they seem normal. Some people can't imagine their lives without lower back pain or headaches or bouts of hyperventilation or wearing a nighttime mouth guard for teeth grinding.

Sweets and caffeine-saturated drinks are just what they do to get through the day. Popping a few pills or having a few drinks has become an accepted way to cope and relax. They have learned to accommodate their stress symptoms, not realizing there are ways to overcome them.

Our bodies and our minds were created to handle a certain amount of strain or tension as a part of living this life. But what happens to a cord when you increase the tension? Even though the cord is designed with a certain amount of give, at some point that cord will break.

We were created with a stress response that was meant to help us recognize and escape danger. We were not created to stay stuck in that stress response. Getting

> God has promised to be with us through times of tension and stress. When stressed, we are meant to say, like Paul:
>
> "WE ARE HARD PRESSED ON EVERY SIDE, BUT NOT CRUSHED; PERPLEXED, BUT NOT IN DESPAIR; PERSECUTED, BUT NOT ABANDONED; STRUCK DOWN, BUT NOT DESTROYED"
> —2 CORINTHIANS 4:8–9

stuck produces the danger of breaking down physically and/or psychologically.

God is our creator and protector. Does this mean we will never have times of stress? No, but God has promised to be with us through times of tension and stress. When stressed, we are meant to say, like Paul did, "We are hard pressed on every side, but not crushed; perplexed, but not in despair; persecuted, but not abandoned; struck down, but not destroyed" (2 Corinthians 4:8–9).

Common Responses *to* Stress

How do we learn to *live with* a stress response without *living in* a stress response? Over my thirty-plus years in counseling, I've seen people become stressed over every imaginable thing or situation under the sun. We are, after all, highly inventive and creative people. But even with all of those variations, I've found that people respond to stress in two basic but different ways: they're either go-getters and stay-putters.

■ THE GO-GETTERS

Go-getters respond to stress by adjusting to its rules, trying to find ways through sheer determination to triumph over stress by getting everything done. They have great plans to do just that. But when they are unable to pull off the impossible, they feel like failures, which increases their stress.

Peter was a classic go-getter. He couldn't remember a life without stress, even from childhood. At an early age, he learned to juggle school, homework, sports, youth groups, volunteer work—whatever

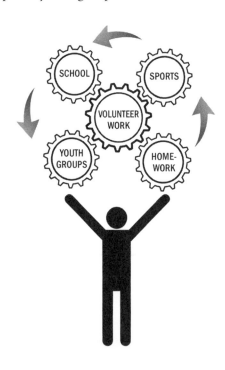

came his way. Energetic and perfectionistic, Peter had energy and stamina that sustained him in a life overcommitted and overscheduled.

Peter knew from an early age that he wanted to be a pilot, and he strove to meet all of the academic and physical requirements for that career. Today was never enough for Peter; he was always reaching, always striving for tomorrow. When he reached one goal, he substituted another, then another.

For Peter, life became less about living and more about accomplishing the goals on his list. People—including his family—were less about relationships and more about contributors to Peter's goals in life. Peter expected life to happen a certain way and doggedly insisted that it did.

When life stopped happening the way it was supposed to, Peter didn't know what to do. When his teenage son didn't listen and became addicted to drugs, Peter didn't know what to do. When Peter's wife threatened to leave him, Peter didn't know what to do. When Peter developed a heart condition, Peter didn't know what to do.

All along, Peter had not realized the stress he had been under or the toll that stress had been taking on his family and his health. Peter had spent his life thinking he could work his way out of any obstacle. The higher the obstacle, the harder he'd had to try. Success was supposed to be a function of how hard he had worked. Now Peter found he was working his way out of his family and working himself to death.

Are you a Go-Getter?

- What are the various responsibilities you're juggling?

- Of the responsibilities you're juggling, which are the ones you *must* attend to? Which are responsibilities you've put on yourself?

- In what ways is your hard work unable to control the things happening in your life?

■ THE STAY-PUTTERS

Bill was a classic stay-putter. Almost thirty, he'd never kept a job for more than a year. In between episodes of work, he found friends to take him in or crashed in his parents' basement. By doing that, Bill was wearing out his welcome just about everywhere, including the basement.

For almost a decade, Bill managed to avoid responsibility by stringing together a series of unrelated online college courses. First he was going to get this degree, then a different degree. As long as he kept changing his major, he avoided questions about graduation. But now he was getting older and the questions wouldn't go away.

If only he could get a degree in online gaming, Bill would be happy. Unable to maintain the discipline to show up for a job, Bill was religious about game time. Only in the virtual world could Bill show any sign of success. There had to be some way to work some money out of his online prowess. He thought about entering a competition, but he

waited too long to sign up. He hadn't even made it to the exhibition hall to watch those who had; instead, he just stayed in the basement and played online games by himself.

Bill was finding it harder and harder to get out of bed in the morning. The stress of each day was becoming too much. He'd always dealt with that stress by not acknowledging it existed and distracting himself with other things. Now those distractions weren't working, and Bill had no idea what he was going to do.

Are you a Stay-Putter?

- What responsibilities are you trying to avoid?

- Put the responsibilities you're avoiding in order of priority so you can focus on them one at a time.

- What distractions are you using to put off making the changes you need to make in your life?

Go-Getters vs. Stay-Putters

If you're a go-getter, you can feel out of control, because while you're in the driver's seat, you've invited a bunch of loud, rowdy stresses to ride with you. These stresses scramble over your seats, push you away from the wheel, and demand you drop everything and take them where they want to go. Stresses can act like a car full of screaming children, wrecking havoc and constantly diverting your attention. You're in the driver's seat of your life, but you don't feel in control.

Stay-putters assign them- selves to the backseat of their lives. Like true backseat drivers, they complain about where they're headed but make no move to switch to the front. Instead, they grumble but go wherever life takes them.

Taking charge of your life means turning over that life to God and his Holy Spirit.

"THE FRUIT OF THE SPIRIT IS LOVE, JOY, PEACE, FORBEARANCE, KINDNESS, GOODNESS, FAITHFULNESS, GENTLENESS AND SELF-CONTROL. AGAINST SUCH THINGS THERE IS NO LAW."
—GALATIANS 5:22-23

Stress is more than happy to drive your life, taking you to places you don't want to go. You can either stay huddled in the backseat, at the mercy of whatever pressure grabs the wheel at any given moment, or you can stop long enough to accept responsibility for your life and decide to drive it yourself. You can either allow a car full of unruly stresses make driving a nightmare or you can stop long enough to get control of your chaos. Either way, you've got to take charge of your life in order to reduce your stress.

GO-GETTERS TRY TO DO IT ALL. STAY-PUTTERS TRY TO DO NOTHING AT ALL.

Go-getters respond to stress by trying to do it all, thinking they can get a handle on stress through sheer productivity. Stay-putters respond to stress by trying to do nothing at all. They try to get a handle on stress through sheer passivity. Neither strategy deals well with stress, because stress builds when you say yes too much and stress builds when you say no too much.

Six Steps
to
Stress Less

In order to stress less, there are six steps you can take that when integrated together provide a pathway to successful, long-term recovery. How do I know? I am privileged to watch this recovery take place in the lives of people all the time.

The six steps to stress less are based on my whole-person approach to recovery, recognizing that a person is made up of different facets. These aspects can combine for good—to promote healing and recovery—or these aspects can combine for bad—to complicate healing and recovery.

As I worked to define and refine my whole-person approach to recovery, I realized applications for a variety of mental health issues, including stress. Over thirty years later, I'm even more convinced about the worth of my approach.

The different facets of a person—the whole-person components—can be addressed together to enhance recovery from stress. When they're working in harmony to reach the goal of healing, recovery has more of a fighting chance at success.

Live Simply

Travis looked at his watch and calculated how long it was going to take to leave work, drive in traffic, pick up the kids, and get them to practice. He could feel his blood pressure rising, which was an additional entry added to his worry list over the past six months.

He hoped his boss, Sandy, wouldn't email him another "emergency" assignment—there were only thirty minutes left in his day. With so many of his tasks already unfinished, Travis had plenty of emergencies to deal with. He just needed to find a way to get out the door on time today. Pam would kill him if the kids were late to practice—again.

When had life become this difficult? There were times when it felt like he could hardly breathe. Forever playing catch-up, he couldn't seem to get a handle on anything.

He just bounced from must-do to must-do without any time in between except to eat—which he was doing too much of according to his doctor—and sleep—which he was doing too little of according to his doctor. Travis hated to admit it, but he felt like he was slipping. He'd always considered himself capable, but now he found himself getting older, fatter, and further behind.

Almost racing to his car, late but hopefully not too late, Travis pulled out of the parking lot and headed toward the freeway. Accelerating up the on-ramp, he found himself day-dreaming what it would be like to keep driving and leave all of it behind, just for a little while.

He was starting to snap at Pam and resent the kids for complicating his life with their endless parade of practices and games and recitals and curriculum nights

and teacher conferences. What he wouldn't give to be left completely alone for forty-eight hours. Lost in those thoughts, Travis almost missed his exit, which would have been a disaster.

■ ■ ■

Travis is someone redlining to the right of overload. Each day brings another task, another duty, another obligation, another requirement, another responsibility. Many people feel like Travis and find themselves drowning under the flood of their own agendas. When asked to evaluate those agendas to see if there is a way to reduce the sheer volume, panic sets in, because each item on the list is stamped "Necessary" in large red letters.

The question to ask, of course, is, this is necessary to whom?

- ■ What a person determines is necessary tells you a great deal about who he or she is.

- ■ What do you find necessary in your life?

- ■ How do you feel about letting go of some of those "necessary" things?

To simplify your life, you need to go through your agendas, priorities, and responsibilities, and determine which ones are truly necessary. Once you've identified the necessary things, you can begin to jettison the rest. However, if you stamp all of your priorities as necessary, then you won't see a way to remove any of them. You'll be right back where you started: more convinced than ever that your life is just one huge pressure after another.

Stop *the* Car

In order to simplify your life, it's time to stop the car and get those obligations under control. You may have invited them along for the ride, but you're still the driver of the car. You can tell some of them to take a hike or, at least, get in the back and stop trying to take the wheel away from you.

> Jesus took time to stop, even with all the truly necessary things he was called to do.
>
> "JESUS OFTEN WITHDREW TO LONELY PLACES AND PRAYED."
> —LUKE 5:16

Did you notice I said to stop the car? Some people are terrified to stop moving. To stop moving means to risk the collective weight of all of their obligations piling up from behind and crushing them. They are convinced that to remain safe, they must stay one step ahead of their obligations. Outrunning is safe; stopping spells disaster.

Stop and take stock of your priorities and your obligations. Stop and take stock of where and how you spend your time. Stop to determine what is *actually* necessary. Stop and carve out time for thought and reflection. Go-getters rarely give themselves permission to stop and reevaluate their activity, resenting anything that retards forward motion. Stay-putters rarely give themselves permission to stop and reevaluate their distractions, resenting anything that smacks of commitment or change or risk.

BOUNCING FROM THING TO THING TO THING MAY PRODUCE A GREAT DEAL OF ACTIVITY, BUT IT RARELY PROMOTES A PATH OF PURPOSE.

What are your goals in life? What are the purposes and priorities that give your life meaning? Bouncing from thing to thing to thing may produce a great deal of activity, but it rarely promotes a path of purpose. Staying hidden from life, huddling in a safe corner, never taking a risk rarely promotes a path of purpose. Without purpose, life is just a series of random

> "GOD IS OUR REFUGE AND STRENGTH, AN EVER-PRESENT HELP IN TROUBLE. THEREFORE WE WILL NOT FEAR, THOUGH THE EARTH GIVE WAY AND THE MOUNTAINS FALL INTO THE HEART OF THE SEA, THOUGH ITS WATERS ROAR AND FOAM AND THE MOUNTAINS QUAKE WITH THEIR SURGING. THE LORD ALMIGHTY IS WITH US; THE GOD OF JACOB IS OUR FORTRESS. HE SAYS, 'BE STILL AND KNOW THAT I AM GOD.'"
> —PSALM 46:1–3, 7, 10

activities, whether you're a go-getter or a stay-putter. What do you want your life to count for?

Actions, as they say, speak louder than words. People act either to create something they desire or to avoid something they fear. What do your actions say about what you desire and what you fear? These are your true priorities.

What happens to gears that are out of alignment? They grind and grate and scrape against each other; gears out of alignment create damage. Too much misalignment, and gears won't operate at all. Compare and contrast what you want your priorities to be and what your priorities actually are. The more out of alignment these are, the more you live at odds with yourself. The more you live at odds with yourself, the more stress you'll have in your life.

Simplifying your life may seem like an exercise in reducing the amount of things you do and, thus, only applicable to go-getters. Simplifying your life, however, is about making sure the things you do have meaning and positive purpose in your life.

Go-getters and stay-putters fill their lives with different amounts of activity but little meaning. Stress is created not merely by doing too many things; stress is created by doing too many of the wrong things and not enough of the right things. Looking at your life through that filter can help you determine what things you need to keep and what things you need to jettison. As Ecclesiastes 3:1, 6 says, "There is a time for everything, . . . a time to keep and a time to throw away." Simple? Yes. Easy? No.

GOD DOES NOT WANT YOU TO LIVE SO BURDENED DOWN BY LIFE THAT YOU MISS OUT ON LIFE.

Taking time to really examine who you are and make changes is not easy. Go-getters think they've got a million better things to do than reflect. Stay-putters recoil from making any sort of commitments or resolutions, convinced that only failure lies ahead. I encourage you to examine your life

GOD DOES NOT WANT YOU TO LIVE SO BURDENED DOWN BY LIFE THAT YOU MISS OUT ON LIFE.

anyway. When you decide that you don't have time to take stock of your life, you have lost control of that life.

Life is about choices. Each yes and each no reveal something about who you are as a person. You can't start to change who you are until you understand who that is. Once you understand who you are, you are better able to bring yourself into alignment with who God wants you to be and how he wants you to live your life. God does not want you to live so burdened down *by* life that you miss out *on* life.

Practice *the* Martha Principle

What I like to call the Martha Principle comes from the story of when Jesus went to visit Martha at her home:

> She had a sister called Mary, who sat at the Lord's feet listening to what he said. But Martha was distracted by all the preparations that had to be made. She came to him and asked, "Lord, don't

you care that my sister has left me to do all the work by myself? Tell her to help me!"

"Martha, Martha," the Lord answered, "you are worried and upset about many things, but few things are needed—or indeed only one. Mary has chosen what is better, and it will not be taken from her" (Luke 10: 39–42).

Only one thing was needed in that moment: stopping and listening to Jesus.

- How often do I get so busy with all of the must-do preparations of my day that I fail to stop and listen to Jesus?

- How often do I get distracted by things that aren't really important and fail to stop and listen to Jesus?

Clearly, Martha's attitude indicated she believed her preparations were necessary—so much so that she had the audacity to give Jesus an order ("Tell her to help me!"). The Martha Principle cautions us that we can become so distracted by our choices that we fail to recognize what is actually important.

Consider the *Whats* and *Whys*

A stress-filled life can cause us to careen from activity to activity or distraction to distraction with little time to stop and think about what we are doing. We are so consumed with the *what* in our lives that we fail to recognize the *why*. Take time to stop and consider all of the *whats* in your life—what you are doing on a regular basis.

On a separate sheet of paper, construct a simple table like the one below. Write each *what* down in the table.

WHATS	WHYS

Next, assign each *what* a *why* and write it down. Then consider how your life would be if you stopped doing that *what*. As much as possible, be truthful and realistic about those consequences.

I hope that through this exercise, you can begin to identify the truly important and necessary things in your life and begin to make choices about what to continue, what to modify (or ask for help accomplishing), and what to end.

ONCE YOU TAKE BACK CONTROL OF THE PRIORITIES IN YOUR LIFE, YOU CAN BEGIN TO REDUCE YOUR STRESS LEVEL.

I encourage you to recognize how much control you have over your choices. Stress has a way of creating its own urgency through manufactured crises. Once you take back control of the priorities in your life, you can begin to reduce your stress level.

Without the false urgency of stress, you'll be able to evaluate when to say yes and when to say no. When each yes or no is in line with the truly important, you'll feel better about and energized by your choices. Life will become less about what you have to do and more about what you want to do.

When you are actively engaged in doing the things that give you purpose and meaning, your life has moments of joy. Saying no to the wrong things and yes to the right things becomes easier. Filled with these moments, stress has less room to maneuver in your life.

Live Within *Your* Means

Simplifying your life is about evaluating the things you do so that you can reduce what isn't necessary or increase what is. Simplifying your life can also be about evaluating the number of things you have and want.

When I was growing up, people didn't talk so much about living simply; people talked about living within their means—not spending more money than you make. In years past, not spending more money than you make meant not spending more money than you brought home.

Today, not spending more money than you make means relying a lot on credit. Many people live with financial stress caused by paying tomorrow for what they want today. This arrangement only works if you're able to keep paying tomorrow. The threat of not being able to pay tomorrow contributes to high levels of stress.

The top two sources of stress for Americans have to

do with money: people worry about their finances in general and about the jobs they have to provide those finances. Living simply for many Americans may mean finding ways to live within their means—reducing their debt, and avoiding living on credit. One article I read put the figure for consumer debt in this country at 11.85 trillion dollars; of that total, 918.5 billion is for credit cards, 8.09 trillion is for mortgages, and 1.19 trillion is for student loans.[4] No wonder so many of us can't sleep at night.

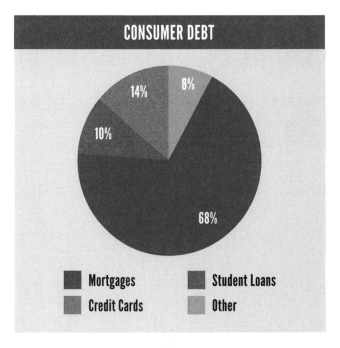

Every household is different, but in order to simplify your life and reduce your stress, you may need to consider how you handle credit and debt. This is especially true if financial concerns are a major source of your stress. The abundance of credit in this country has allowed us to obtain more material goods and services than we are able to immediately pay for. There is no doubt we are wealthy people. However, for all of our wealth, we are not at peace.

For many of us, living simply may mean living with less—with fewer things *and* less stress.

For many of us, living simply may mean living with less—with fewer things and less stress.

"THE SLEEP OF A LABORER IS SWEET, WHETHER THEY EAT LITTLE OR MUCH, BUT AS FOR THE RICH, THEIR ABUNDANCE PERMITS THEM NO SLEEP."
—ECCLESIASTES 5:12

Live Organized

The ding on her cell phone startled her. Puzzled, Beth wondered why she was getting a reminder. Reading the short text, her heart sank. She'd completely forgotten about the meeting. She'd agreed to help Kathy weeks ago but only because she felt guilty. Beth didn't really want to go to the meeting, let alone stay and help Kathy clean up. This was going to put her seriously behind. Tonight was the night she was supposed to catch up on all the things she hadn't done over the weekend, like laundry and buying that baby gift.

One small ding and Beth felt close to tears. There was too much going on, too much she had to do. She never caught a break, never got caught up. Beth prided herself on being the go-to person, someone people could rely on, which is why so many people asked her to do things.

Didn't they understand how much pressure she was under? Now all she wanted to do was run and hide. Lately, she wasn't motivated to do anything, which is why last weekend came and went without the laundry getting done and the baby gift being purchased.

Beth had thought she would have time tonight to find some breathing room. Now time had run out—all because of this stupid meeting. She resented losing her evening and resented Kathy for having pressured her into saying yes in the first place. Checking the time, Beth started planning how to get out of the crisis. Forget the laundry; she'd make do.

Tomorrow was the baby shower and Beth had desperately wanted to find the perfect gift. Well, so much for the perfect gift; that would take time she didn't have. If she shopped through lunch, maybe, just maybe, she could find something acceptable to pop in a gift bag. Janice would just have to be happy with whatever she got; after all, it was a gift. Beth figured she'd put a gift receipt in the bag and if Janice didn't like the gift, she could just take her own time to go back to the store and get something better.

Time always seemed to be running out and Beth always seemed to be running after it. When, she wondered, was she ever going to get caught up?

■ ■ ■

Stress is not the ideal environment to make the best decisions. Stress skews your priorities and downsizes goals. Desperate, you make short-term decisions that have long-term consequences. Pressure starts to poison even the best of intentions.

However, knowing what your priorities are and the goals you want to work to achieve allows you to take control of your time. In a way, this is similar to keeping a financial budget, which is one of the ways people have in order to gain control over their money. The budget defines the financial obligations a person has and allocates money to satisfy those obligations, starting with the most basic needs of food, clothing, and shelter.

The budget also helps create parameters for how the money coming in each month will advance a person's financial goals. Without a budget, many people come to the end of the month and wonder, *Where did all the money go?*

> Without a budget, many people come to the end of the month and wonder, Where did all the money go?
>
> "CAST BUT A GLANCE AT RICHES, AND THEY ARE GONE, FOR THEY WILL SURELY SPROUT WINGS AND FLY OFF TO THE SKY LIKE AN EAGLE."
> —PROVERBS 23:5

With our fast-paced society, some people consider time the new currency. Time, therefore, can be very similar to money. Without an intentional plan for how to use your time, you may wind up at the end of a day, a week, a month, a year, or a lifetime and wonder, *Where did all the time go?*

There is great value in financial management and there is great value in time management. Another way to characterize time management is to live organized. A budget can help your money work for you; living organized can help your time work for you.

In the last chapter, we talked about simplifying your life so that you can cut down on the stress of misaligned priorities. In this chapter, we're going to talk about organizing your life so that you cut down on the stress of mistimed priorities.

Manage *Your* Time

What do think of when you hear the phrase *time management*? If you are a go-getter, you may hear those words and think of how many tasks you can cram into a single day. However, I didn't say *task* management; I said *time* management. Healthy time management, meant to reduce stress and increase quality of life, includes more than merely scheduling tasks. Time management means incorporating times to accomplish tasks, yes, but also times of rest, reflection, recreation, and communication. Each of these is needed daily to advance priorities and goals.

If you are a stay-putter, you may hear "time management" and think of how impossible it is for you to get anything done, no matter how much time you have. For you, time management means incorporating effort, progress, completion, and accomplishment into each day in order to advance priorities and goals.

Time—no matter how much of it you have—needs to be harnessed and controlled: each morning (or even the night before), decide what your goals and priorities are for the day. If the day is a work day, then arriving to work on time and being ready to actively participate are going to be main priorities.

However, most people don't work sixteen-hour days, so there will be hours in each day for other activities. Decide ahead of time what those activities should be based upon what you want to accomplish as well as on the type of person you want to be.

For example, as you're on your way to work, you might decide to listen to music or an informative or informational podcast. You might decide to spend the time in quiet reflection, meditation, or prayer, depending upon your mode of transport. At lunch, you might send a quick text or place a quick call to a friend or family member. On your way home, you might catch up on the news and take time to disconnect from your workday. If you don't intentionally plan your day, your day will plan you.

> If you don't intentionally plan your day, your day will plan you.

> "WHATEVER YOU DO, WHETHER IN WORD OR DEED, DO ALL IN THE NAME OF THE LORD JESUS, GIVING THANKS TO GOD THE FATHER THROUGH HIM."
> —COLOSSIANS 3:17

If the day is not a workday, then you will have more time to harness and manage. There is a danger in thinking that you have all the time in the world over the weekend, but how many Sundays (or the equivalent) have you gone to bed, realizing you didn't get done half of what you had wanted. Instead of being satisfied with goals accomplished, you're distressed about tasks left undone. Now not only do you have the week ahead, but you're also playing catch-up from the week just ended.

When it comes to time management, the challenge for go-getters is to balance time with reflection. The challenge for stay-putters is to balance time with achievement.

Downsize *Your* Stuff

At a certain point in my life, I came to realize that I didn't so much own my stuff as my stuff owned me.

- First of all, the more stuff I had, the more energy and effort I put into maintaining and housing the stuff.

- Second of all, the more stuff I wanted, the more energy and effort I put into obtaining the stuff, which brought me back to the first point.

In our culture, we are constantly told we must have this or that. We are told these things are necessary. So we spend energy, effort, time, and money obtaining, maintaining, and housing all this stuff, which erodes the energy, effort, time, and money we have for other aspects of our lives. This stuff ends up extracting collateral cost beyond just what we paid for it. We invest so much to get and hold on to this stuff.

Then, over time, we see how fleeting and unsatisfying getting and holding on to this stuff really is. We conclude this stuff isn't all that valuable after all. We realize we've put in all this effort for all this stuff, without real benefit, leaving us disillusioned and dissatisfied. So what do we tend to do? Go buy more stuff!

TAKE BACK CONTROL FROM YOUR STUFF!

What's the answer? Take back control from your stuff! Have you ever watched one of those shows about hoarding on TV? Usually, the shows involve people who have become inundated with stuff. For hoarders, every room gets packed to the brim with things—so much so, you can hardly see the floor. There are stacks and piles of items upon items, most of which are impossible to use, because they're impossible to get to. The house ceases to be a home and becomes a glorified storage unit.

During these shows, professionals are brought in to help the person go through and sort the stuff, generally into three piles: keep, throw, and donate. Talk about simple.

1. Keep the most important.

2. Donate to someone else in need.

3. Throw away the rest.

If you've ever watched one of these shows, you know this simple exercise can be excruciatingly difficult, especially for those with tendencies to hoard.

Downsizing your stuff allows you to see—and use—those items that are truly meaningful to you. Instead of having five salad bowls, you use and enjoy the one you inherited from a beloved aunt. Instead of gathering dust in an out-of-reach corner of a forgotten cabinet, that bowl is front and center, a beautiful reminder of her love and affection. And those four other bowls? They can be donated to an organization that will sell them to help the disadvantaged. How can that not be a win-win?

Have you ever moved from a smaller home to a larger living space? When you first moved in, you were probably amazed at how much room you had. How long did it take before that room got filled up?

Have you ever moved from a larger home to a smaller one? How hard was it to downsize? We become attached to things, even things we don't use. I encourage you to let some of these things go, so they can find their way to someone who might truly need them. Most important, those things will no longer be your responsibility. You can let them go and simplify your life.

Clear *Your* Clutter

As you downsize your stuff, it's important to go through all the areas of your house, not just those out-of-the-way cabinets, closets, and drawers. You will also want to find ways to clear your clutter. When you come home, how can you relax when your countertops, tables, couches, chairs, and/or desks are piled with disordered things? How are you supposed to find what you need in all that?

Many organization specialists counsel people to create what the specialists call white spaces. A white space is an area in a room that is simple and devoid of clutter. In a corner of your living room, you might place a chair with a small table and a single lamp. No knickknacks, no plants, no magazines—nothing on that table but the lamp. Your eye is given a break from stimulation. The space becomes a calming visual retreat.

Clearing your clutter means going through your personal spaces and removing extraneous items. Certainly keep those things that give you special delight, but realistically, how many little bobbles can you keep track of? Can thirty of the same thing really be as fulfilling as one or two? If a collection of some item is special to you, instead of displaying all thirty, why not put out one or two

> Making choices is a way for you to take back control.
>
> "LIKE A CITY WHOSE WALLS ARE BROKEN THROUGH IS A PERSON WHO LACKS SELF-CONTROL."
> —PROVERBS 25:28

and then rotate them during the year? As a practical matter, one or two things are much easier to dust than thirty. Your personal spaces need to be crafted to relieve stress, not produce it.

Use *the* Three Bs

Life can be messy, however, and not every house can or should look like one of those perfectly staged model homes. We have stuff, our spouses have stuff, and our kids really have stuff. How are we supposed to find white space within all that stuff?

Ask a professional organizer and you'll probably hear a variation on the three Bs: baskets, boxes, and bags. Instead of having magazines and circulars scattered across every conceivable surface so that you run from room to room to room, trying to remember where you last saw the one you want, designate a basket in a main room to put them in. As the basket gets full, clear out the old magazines to make room for the new. If you must keep for reference all twelve issues of a monthly magazine, store them in a magazine binder, a box, or a magazine holder in a closet. You don't have to physically see every item you have to know where each is.

Are you catching the theme here? Simplifying your life requires intentionality and choices. A simple fact is you cannot do it all. Another simple fact is you cannot keep it all. Trying to do either or both complicates your life, adding to your stress. Making choices is a way for you to take back control.

Practice *the* One Out, One In Rule

A word of caution here: simplifying your life is not a one-and-done affair. Stuff and clutter don't stop just because you've (finally) got some sort of control over your life. They keep coming. In order to maintain your balance, I suggest before you say yes to another must-have thing, decide what you would give up to make room for the new thing. If you're not willing to give up what you've got for whatever it is you want, say no. Say no, out of a sense of peace, instead of a sense of distress. When your life is already full and satisfied,

you won't miss whatever that new thing is. However, if you determine this whatever-it-is is worth rearranging your life for, let go of something less important to make room for the whatever-it-is.

BEFORE YOU SAY YES TO ANOTHER MUST-HAVE THING, DECIDE WHAT YOU WOULD GIVE UP TO MAKE ROOM FOR THE NEW THING.

This example of the one out, one in rule applies not just to things but also to tasks and obligations. Before you say yes to the PTA president or yes to that softball league or yes to the library board, decide if you need to give something up to make room in your schedule. If your

schedule is already packed with obligations that give you pleasure and purpose, don't feel bad about saying no to something new.

If this is something you really want to do but don't have the time, instead of saying no, say not now. Then determine how to create room in your schedule in the future. Perhaps you have an obligation that has a natural end date and you can use that transition to take on the new task.

Remember, saying yes to too many things means you're not really saying yes, because you won't have the time or the energy to truly put forth your best for each obligation. The things you say yes to should deserve your time and attention.

Use *Your* Head *to* Plan Ahead

Too many of us live our lives in perpetual crises. Although we've known for three months that our in-laws were coming to visit over the holidays, we end up in full-blown panic the weekend before. We blame our spouses for having parents; we rant at our kids for the state of their rooms, which have been that way since Easter; we determine we must redo the plumbing in the hall bathroom, which has leaked for a year and a half. Simply put, by procrastinating, we often create our own unnecessary whirlwinds of panic and stress.

I've worked with some people who swore they needed this kind of motivation to get anything done. Such an attitude is a choice, not some sort of genetic predisposition (like to a disease) or innate characteristic (like the length of your tibia). Desperation should not be the driver in getting you motivated. If you choose to allow this, you choose to continue a stressful, panic-driven life.

Instead, use your head to plan ahead. If you know you're going to have company over the holidays and that bathroom really needs to get fixed, don't procrastinate. Schedule time to do the work yourself, if you are so inclined and capable. Or hire a plumber. If you need to hire someone, planning ahead allows you to have the time to research options and you'll probably make a better choice and spend less money. Last-minute plumbers tend to cost more.

PLAN FOR THE UNEXPECTED.

What if your in-laws call unexpectedly and decide to just drop in? How can you plan for events like that? The answer is to plan for the unexpected. Instead of waiting until you've got company confirmed before you clean your house, clean your house regularly. That way, if someone does drop by unannounced, you can straighten up quickly and not stress about your company seeing your three-day-old laundry still piled on the kitchen table.

Using your head to plan ahead is really a variation of using a budget for your money. If you know that tires get bald and kids outgrow clothes, then planning ahead for these normal events keeps them from landing in the crisis category. The fewer crises you have in your life, the less stress you'll feel. Life has enough stresses of its own without your contributing to that number by failing to plan for what you already know is coming.

Unplug

I'm old enough to remember the promises made upon the dawn of technology. Each new tech device was supposed to make our lives simpler. We were supposed to have more time. I don't know about you, but there are many days when I feel I have less.

> There are times I simply need to do a tech detox and unplug myself.
>
> "BY THE SEVENTH DAY GOD HAD FINISHED THE WORK HE HAD BEEN DOING; SO ON THE SEVENTH DAY HE RESTED FROM ALL HIS WORK."
> —GENESIS 2:2

Before these technological innovations, there were two ways to get a hold of me—in person or by phone. Now I have multiple phone numbers, multiple email accounts, and multiple websites. I'm on Facebook and Twitter. The number of contacts I manage daily has literally exploded. I've got devices that beep and ding and ping and ring, each one demanding my attention.

I write and speak about the dark side of technology frequently; yet I dearly love my tech. I love it so much, I need to constantly be on guard that I don't love it more than my wife and my kids. I love it so much, I need to constantly be on guard that I don't get distracted by my tech and neglect my responsibilities. There are times I simply need to do a tech detox and unplug myself. I try to set aside one day a week when I'm unplugged from technology, although

> "IF YOU KEEP YOUR FEET FROM BREAKING THE SABBATH AND FROM DOING AS YOU PLEASE ON MY HOLY DAY, IF YOU CALL THE SABBATH A DELIGHT AND THE LORD'S HOLY DAY HONORABLE, AND IF YOU HONOR IT BY NOT GOING YOUR OWN WAY AND NOT DOING AS YOU PLEASE OR SPEAKING IDLE WORDS, THEN YOU WILL FIND YOUR JOY IN THE LORD."
> —ISAIAH 58:13–14

a part of me still tried to argue that I'm too busy to give up an entire day. When that happens, it helps to remember that even God took a day off (Genesis 2:2).

As a Christian and as a counselor, I believe taking a day of rest each week is important. Physically, I need the rest. Emotionally, I need the break. Relationally, I need to spend undivided time with family and friends. Spiritually, I need to put God's priorities above my own. When I have all of these things in alignment, I am less stressed and more at peace.

We have more control over our lives than we think. When we say we have to do something or something must be done, we give agreement to that imperative. Do most of us have to work? Yes, we do. Providing for ourselves and any who depend upon us is an imperative. However, as I said before, there are more hours in our days and weeks than just working and sleeping. During those hours, we can either choose to give in to the urgency of stress or we can reclaim those hours by taking back control. How we choose to use that time reflects our priorities and our goals. The choice, though difficult, is simple. For less stress, choose to be well aligned and well organized.

STEP #3

Live Healthy

Dan, a colleague of mine, was one of those people who prided himself on his ability to always say yes. Dan was able to keep this up for years, until things began to break down:

> I [Dan] was strong physically and mentally. I knew I was pushing the envelope with the intensity of my work, but I was confident—stubbornly cocky might be a better way to say it—that *I* could make a success of it, even though I was counseling people with the same tendencies toward burning the candle at both ends while I looked for creative ways to burn it in the middle also. I lived in full denial that I, too, might have a problem.

> Then, as it happens with so many people, I crossed that invisible line between living a whole,

healthy life and what I would probably now call "temporary insanity." Not in the clinical sense, perhaps, but certainly a life that was out of control to the point of not knowing who I was, where I was, or what I was doing.

I started drinking on weekends. Not much at first; just enough to take away the tension. The alcohol numbed my hurts, even as it numbed my spirit. I had crossed the line.

I had once been regular at church but now had quit. My friends assumed I'd dropped off the face of the earth. If it hadn't been for my wife, who hung in there with me, there's no telling what might have happened. I assigned her as the "designated worshiper," while I stayed home and drank. It became obvious to me later that she had her own needs, and her presence in a house of worship eventually became the turning point in her own life and relationship with God.

I quit exercising—something I'd enjoyed for years. I stopped running, let the bicycles gather dust, put on a paunch, and didn't even care. I quit paying attention to what was important in my life, and I wasn't prepared to accept responsibility for my deteriorating condition. It had to be my circumstances, my workload, unfair people, the government . . . my blame list was endless. The only problem with my list was that my name wasn't on it. Big mistake.

■ ■ ■

In my presentation to audiences on the whole-person approach to recovery, I'll invariably talk about diet and exercise. Looking out over the faces in the audience, I've seen some of them just turn me off like a switch. Sure, they came to learn how to recover from challenges in their lives, like stress, but how dare I suggest they get off the couch and put down the cookies! After all, they want to feel better—not worse!

I'll ask the audience to tell me what the word *exercise* means to them. Of course, there are those who give positive responses, but they are often drowned out by the negative ones:

- "I hate it."

- "No fun."

- "I have no time."

- "Exercise is work."

- "Not for me."

- "I know I should, but it's just a pain."

- "I can't lose weight anyway, so why try?"

- "I joined two fitness clubs, and that didn't work."

- At one seminar, a man joked, "I hire other people to work out for me."

The E Word: Exercise

According to the latest information from the Centers for Disease Control and Prevention, about half of American adults met the physical activity guidelines for aerobic activity, while just over one in five of us met both the aerobic and muscle strengthening guidelines.[5] However, a lack of exercise is not the result of a lack of information. We've been hearing the drumbeat for years; we simply choose not to listen.

For those of you who view *exercise* as a dirty word, allow me to suggest a different viewpoint, one from my friend Covert Bailey. He brings more fun and frolic to the subject of fitness than anyone I've met over the years. I love what he says:

> Start so slowly that people make fun of you. . . . Gentle exercise pays off. If you are exercising at a slow pace, one that is only 65 percent of your

maximum heart rate, say, your body will adapt and profit from the exercise. If you're just walking, it may not seem like much to you or your friends, but at night, as you sleep, your body will say, "Boy, she doesn't exercise very hard, but she sure does a lot of it. I'd better adapt to this."[6]

Covert is right, of course. When you begin "so slowly that people make fun of you," might I suggest you do it with a friend? Not one who is too fit though—that might discourage you from ever exercising again. Instead, start walking, hiking, or biking with someone who's not out to shatter an Olympic record.

Make your exercise fun, but at the same time don't stop at every other house to chat with a neighbor and have a cup of coffee. Maintain a gentle but steady pace as you talk with your friend, listen to music, smell the flowers, and/or enjoy some scenery you may not have noticed for years.

You really do need to engage in some form of exercise several times a week to help cope with stress. Exercise does not require running marathons or deadlifting three hundred pounds. Exercise is not extreme skiing, two-hundred-mile cycling events, or Ironman competitions. Exercise can be as simple as a ten-minute walk twice a day, going on a bike ride, or playing a little tennis. Before you know it, you'll be doing your activity for twenty or thirty minutes, perhaps even an hour.

MAKE YOUR EXERCISE FUN!

CDC guidelines for adults 18–64 are for 150 minutes (two and a half hours) per week of moderate-intensity exercise (like brisk walking) and two days per week of muscle-strengthening exercises.[7] If you make it fun, you won't even look at your watch.

Until now you may have been too busy to exercise, because you thought exercise had to be drudgery. Here's the good news: You *can* slow down and enjoy the flowers. You *can* direct your energy toward health (with less available for stress). When you do, you will find yourself one step closer to regaining control of your life.

The D Word: Diet

If "exercise" is the *E* word, then "diet" is the *D* word. We know we need to exercise and we know we need to eat healthy. Stress does not assist either of those good intentions. Stress makes you so tired, you don't have energy to exercise. Stress creates such an atmosphere of panic and depletion, you run to the wrong types of foods to make you feel better. Remember that eating too much or eating unhealthy foods was reported by a third of us when we're stressed.

Sally came to me overweight, unhappy, and consumed by stress. The more stressed out she felt, the worse she ate. Food had become her "happy place," the one source of guaranteed comfort in a difficult, sometimes painful life. The more weight she put on, the guiltier and more stressed she felt about the weight. The more weight she put on, the harder she found moving became. Her joints hurt; her back hurt. She felt lousy much of the time and had no energy. Caught in this cycle, she was overwhelmed by even thinking about how to escape.

Together, Sally and I worked to come up with a plan she could live with:

> One . . . I [Sally] started eating a simple, healthy breakfast each morning. That was my only guideline . . . that it had to be healthy. No list of

special foods, no restrictive diet, no calories to count, lie about, or eat. Nothing. What surprised me was that I was being asked to make my *own* decisions and not rely on someone else's idea of what I should consume. I was given complete freedom to eat when I wanted and how much I wanted. It just had to be healthy. Actually, this frightened me, because I wanted to be told what to do.

So I chose to eat a large breakfast of whole grain cereal and low-fat milk and some fruit each morning. It was bulky, so it made me feel full. It wasn't sugary, so my insulin level did not increase. I knew all about this theoretically, but it wasn't easy to put into practice. A big part of me (which was most of me) hated it. At first I missed my usual two jelly donuts and three cups of coffee

with lots of cream, followed in a few minutes by grazing in the fridge for a few leftovers from the night before. But I'd made an agreement with Dr. Jantz to do this, and besides I was desperate.

The second thing was even more amazing to me. I was asked not to weigh myself at all in between sessions. I'd already sent my scale "on vacation," so there was no way to weigh myself at home. But I was not to weigh myself *anywhere*. This was difficult. How would I know if I was making any progress if I couldn't weigh myself two or three times a day as I'd done most of my life? I didn't understand it, but I said I'd stick with the program and obey the rules.[8]

Some of us grew up with mothers who loved to prepare big fattening sack lunches for us to eat at school. The sandwiches were works of art, prepared on soft slices of enriched white bread, overlaid with greasy salami, bologna, and thick layers of mayonnaise and butter. Nestled in the bottom of the bag would be a love note accompanied by two or three large freshly baked chocolate or peanut butter cookies. Our mothers may have had the best of intentions for us, but those good wishes later may have brought on disaster as we struggled with our weight, which contributed to our mounting stress.

Simply put, a healthy body is able to handle the normal demands of life. When you fail to consistently give your body the nutrients it needs, you place the body under stress. When you feed your body foods that aren't healthy, you place your body under stress.

BEGIN THE SHIFT FROM EATING UNHEALTHY TO FEEL BETTER TO EATING BETTER TO FEEL HEALTHY.

Behavior patterns can contribute to stress, thought patterns can contribute to stress, and eating patterns can contribute to stress. Excessive stress leaches your body of energy and resiliency. As you work to overcome and reduce the stress in your life, you'll want to start feeding your body differently. Begin the shift from eating unhealthy to feel better to eating better to feel healthy.

Read food labels more carefully and seek to interpret the wealth of information they contain. This is a far cry from the ineffective calorie counting and roller-coaster dieting you may have engaged in before. Healthy eating isn't complicated:

- Eat whole foods instead of processed foods: vegetables and fruits, whole-grain breads, lean meats, and dairy (if you aren't intolerant to dairy)

- Use moderate amounts of healthy fats, like flaxseed, olive, and canola oils.

- Significantly reduce the amount of processed sugar you consume. I think you'll find that the less refined sugar you have, the less you crave it.

- Take a good, bio-available multivitamin and mineral nutritional supplement.

- Drink more water—just water. You can add a piece of fruit for some flavor.

Sally had to learn that dieting and bingeing were terrible obstacles to her stressed physical health and mental stability. When she finally understood that dieting and bingeing were making her more prone to stress-related illnesses, heart and kidney disease, and stroke, she knew she had to make a change. To do this, Sally had to start listening to her body. She had actually forgotten what it was like to eat normally.

THE ONLY WAY TO GET A DIFFERENT RESULT IS TO TRY SOMETHING DIFFERENT.

In the past, she had engaged in so much secret eating, squirreling away money for snacks, and hoarding of food that she no longer knew what it was like to eat food to provide nourishment and strength for her body. Though change was a struggle, Sally slowly substituted healthy choices for unhealthy habits. She not only lost weight, she also gained insight about herself that she was able to use in other areas of her life.

Prying your hands off the donut box or coaxing yourself off the couch can seem like tremendous effort, especially when you're convinced they are essential to coping with the stress in your life. On the contrary, they are contributing to your stress by weighing you down and wearing you out. You cannot win over stress with that strategy. The only way to get a different result is to try something different. Talk to your doctor and develop a plan to change the way you eat and increase your activity level. I promise you, you'll feel better, be less stressed and be more optimistic about life.

Live Present

I was raised in Dodge City, Kansas. Located on the Arkansas River, Dodge City was settled in 1872 and soon became a notorious frontier town and cattle-shipping point on the Santa Fe Trail. Of course, all this was long before my arrival. By the time I was born, Dodge City was actively reliving its legendary past, through historic preservation and Wild West reenactments. The Arkansas River flowed through the center of town, and as a child I thought that river was the largest, longest, most dangerous body of water on earth. The Old West buildings on Front Street seemed enormous to me—silent witnesses of past gunfights. Boot Hill was still there and, to a child, Dodge City was bigger than life.

I remember the first time I returned home as an adult. I went down to the Arkansas River and thought, *What's so big about this trickling body of water? In the state of Washington, we'd call it a stream.* Then I walked over to Front Street and thought, *It's so small. Where are all those tall buildings that used to be here?* Even the reenactments of the gunfights seemed like something out of a B movie.

Just about everything was—and is—pretty small in Dodge City, Kansas. As a boy, I saw the city and its legendary history through the eyes of a child. When I returned, nothing had changed except my perspective. I had put away my childish perspective and had begun to see Dodge City through adult eyes.

What do you think would happen if you revisited some of the old ghost towns that haunt your memories? One of your ghost towns probably isn't Dodge City, Kansas. But one of your ghost towns might be

SOMETIMES THE LIFE WE LIVE CAUSES STRESS AND SOMETIMES THE LIFE WE LIVED CAUSES STRESS.

- the house where you grew up and were taught you weren't a capable person.

- the school where you were taunted and teased and picked last.

- a person not a place—a person who withheld approval and affection, though you did everything you could to earn them.

Sometimes the life we live causes stress and sometimes the life we *lived* causes stress. Each of us is a product of our past. If that past is full of ghosts, that past will haunt the present. To determine if memories of your past are creating stress in your present, ask yourself the following questions:

1. What negative memories seem to haunt me? Which events and the pain they caused are still vivid, as though they just happened?

2. What words or voices from the past are still ringing in my mind today?

> You will have to make a daily decision to dismiss the hurtful memories of the past and concentrate on the positive things of today, until the past no longer controls your thoughts.
>
> "WE KNOW THAT IN ALL THINGS GOD WORKS FOR THE GOOD OF THOSE WHO LOVE HIM, WHO HAVE BEEN CALLED ACCORDING TO HIS PURPOSE."
> —ROMANS 8:28

If you find that past pain still has power over you today, you need to begin moving out of your past and into the present. Start moving out of your ghost towns by reminding yourself those days are over. You may have had no power to stop them negatively affecting your past, but you do have the power to keep them from negatively affecting your present. Even more, God has the power to redeem those negative events and turn them into good.

Think about the good things of the present and be thankful for them. Think about each of your abilities and gifts and how each has played a part in making you the unique person you are. You will have to make a daily decision to dismiss the hurtful memories of the past and concentrate on the positive things of today, until the past no longer controls your thoughts.

The choice is yours. It will require some risk and demand a deeper trust of yourself and of God, but that will only enhance your growth. In the end, all you will lose are your ghosts of the past. What you will gain is an opportunity to regain control of your life.

We all have the capacity to become what we were meant—created—to be. Our ghosts haunt us and keep us fearful. God means for us, through his power, to break free from the past. Do you believe God has the power and desire to do that for you? Can you say, like the apostle Paul, "Forgetting what is behind and straining toward what is ahead, I press on toward the goal to win the prize for which God has called me heavenward in Christ Jesus" (Philippians 3:13–14)?

Acknowledge *Your* Ghosts *from the* Past

In order to forget something, you have to first acknowledge what that something is. You can't forget what you won't admit you know.

> When Debbie came to work with me, she couldn't forget her past, because she consistently refused to acknowledge it. A classic overachiever, Debbie felt like her life was coming apart at the seams. Nothing was turning out the way she had envisioned it, and the stress of failure and disappointment threatened to drown her.

> Her physician had done what she could medically, but much of Debbie's stress was self-generated. Though Debbie considered the need for counseling one more failure on her part, she nonetheless had nowhere else to turn. Debbie was supposed to be better than this, stronger than this, more competent than this. Debbie was furious with herself and with her "weakness" and wasn't

shy about spreading that anger to the other person in the room—me.

One source of her anger at me was my persistence in talking about her past. Debbie was convinced her problems were in her present and had nothing to do with her past. The past was the past, and Debbie was determined to keep it buried. She had no idea how haunted she was by her own ghosts of a disapproving mother, an emotionally distant father, and a rebellious older sister. These ghosts haunted Debbie's present, propelling her to seek approval and value through what she accomplished, instead of for who she was, which, to Debbie, was never good enough.

YOU CAN'T FORGET WHAT YOU WON'T ADMIT YOU KNOW.

"You can't let go of the past," I told her, "until you acknowledge you're holding on to it. You can't forget what you won't admit you know." Debbie found it painful to admit what she knew—that none of her family had been able to give her the love she needed growing up.

- Her mother had been awash in such personal negativity that Debbie could make no headway toward approval.

- Her father had been so disappointed in having girls instead of boys that he ceded their raising to their mother and concentrated his efforts on work.

- Her sister had rebelled against these attitudes and turned her energies to waging war on her parents, with no cease-fire possible to consider her younger sister.

Debbie thought she was living in the present, but in truth, her present was overshadowed by her past. Until Debbie acknowledged this past, she couldn't let it go.

Living in the past is stressful because you end up trying to change something that's already happened. Understanding your past and how your past has and is affecting you is crucial to living in the present. When you identify the ghosts, you are able to banish them and move on. Once Debbie realized how much the past was pressuring her present decisions and actions, she was able to make changes. Together, we evaluated her attitudes and activities and worked to bring them into alignment with who she was in the present and who she wanted to be in the future.

LIVING IN THE PAST IS STRESSFUL BECAUSE YOU END UP TRYING TO CHANGE SOMETHING THAT'S ALREADY HAPPENED.

Banish *Your* Past Ghosts *from the* Present

In the city of Carmel, California, there is a famous cypress tree, weathered and gnarled and growing out of solid rock on the edge of the rugged coast. If that cypress could talk, it might complain about the coastal storms that have battered it for so many years, twisting its branches. It might curse those who maliciously carved initials on its weather-beaten trunk. In spite of all that, the tree remains a lasting symbol of great beauty, the object of photographers worldwide, and a visual representation of tenacity and courage against the ravages of nature.

The challenges of your life have shaped you, requiring tenacity and courage. Some of you may have wrenching, terrible memories. I just want to remind you that you did not always have control over what happened to you. In fact, most of your early life experiences may have been completely out of your control, which gives you even greater reason to view your earlier challenges from a fresh perspective and to see the past with adult eyes, taking note of your struggles in a light that will enhance your growth, give you hope for your better future, and bring greater healing and less stress.

However, some past pain can be so deeply embedded, you need to be willing to ask for help. If your past includes verbal, psychological, physical, or sexual abuse, you will need help in healing from that pain. Recovery from those particular situations requires the skilled knowledge of a professional counselor. So often, abuse creates a sense of isolation for the victim, with shame and guilt creating walls to keep out others and hide the secret. You do not need to walk this journey alone. Healing is not your sole responsibility and asking for help is not failure. Telling your story will not destroy you; telling your story will free you.

If much of your stress comes from the ghosts from your past, you must acknowledge those ghosts, so you can banish them and remove their power over you. The

We must live our lives in the present and stop turning over our present to the past.

"FORGET THE FORMER THINGS; DO NOT DWELL ON THE PAST. SEE, I AM DOING A NEW THING! NOW IT SPRINGS UP; DO YOU NOT PERCEIVE IT? I AM MAKING A WAY IN THE WILDERNESS AND STREAMS IN THE WASTELAND."
—ISAIAH 43:18-19

past is gone; the future is not guaranteed. What we are given is today. And because we are just given today, we must live our lives in the present and stop turning over our present to the past.

THE PAST IS GONE; THE FUTURE IS NOT GUARANTEED. WHAT WE ARE GIVEN IS TODAY.

Today and every day, in each situation you find yourself in, you have a choice. Acknowledging a painful past so that you can truly let it go will not be easy. However, making that choice will be worth the effort. Once you understand your past, you can put it behind you and run the race God has set for you, unhindered by ghosts.

STEP #5

Live Grace-Full

Jean didn't have much of a relationship with her mother. Growing up, Jean didn't remember her mother putting in much of an effort to get along and, truthfully, once Jean hit puberty, she hadn't either. She resented a mother who always seemed so tired and stressed out and defensive about everyone and everything, even Jean. As a young child, Jean had tried to make things right for her mother by being as good as she could be. When that proved unsuccessful, Jean stopped trying to be perfect and started trying to be invisible.

As soon as she could, Jean began to establish distance between herself and her mother. She stayed out of her mother's way as a child and stayed several states away as an adult. Yet for all of that distance, Jean's mother was never far from Jean. She'd hear her mother's voice in her head when she was stressed. She could see her mother's look of disapproval when she failed. Try as she might, Jean found that her mother still shadowed her life. Jean vividly remembered the day she realized just how close she still was to her mother.

That day was full of stress, with too much to do and too little time, including potty training her daughter, Emily. Jean had been trying to accomplish the chore of potty training over the past several weeks, frustrated that Emily just wasn't getting it. On that day, an exasperated Jean, juggling three things at once, set the toddler in front of the television to watch a cartoon, so she (Jean) could, finally, get something—anything—done.

WHEN YOU HAVE TOO MUCH TO DO, ANY REQUEST BECOMES UNREASONABLE.

Jean was already tense, frustrated, and on edge when it happened: Emily had an accident, which couldn't have come at a worse time. On top of an already stressful day, Jean now had to also deal with soiled pants and a stained couch. Jean was convinced that Emily had known she needed to go but had deliberately chosen to stay on that couch to watch the cartoon.

Furious, Jean jerked Emily up from the couch and carried her straight-armed to the bathroom, setting her down hard on the toilet. Along the way, she berated her two-year-old for her disobedience. When Emily burst into tears of despair, Jean felt strangely satisfied with her daughter's distress. After all, Emily's deliberate actions had caused Jean's distress. Why shouldn't her daughter share in that pain? Then a wave of realization hit Jean. Her mother had always seemed to smirk whenever Jean was distressed. She remembered how much that hurt her, to think her mother took some sort of pleasure from her own pain. Now here she was doing the very same thing—and to a two-year-old! How could this have happened? How could Jean have turned into her mother?

◼ ◼ ◼

When stress takes over your life, two-year-olds become adversaries. When you have too much to do, any request becomes unreasonable—no matter who makes it. When you have too little time, any demand on your time becomes a demand you resent. Stress has a way of reordering the us-versus-them columns. Jean grew up with a stressed-out mother who's "us" category really came down to "me." "Them" was defined as everyone else, including Jean.

When the world is against you, when people are out to get you, when events are against you, you live in a state of siege. A siege mentality contributes to the state of Red Alert talked about earlier. Unresolved anger is a breeding ground for stress.

> Unresolved anger is a breeding ground for stress.
>
> "GET RID OF ALL BITTERNESS, RAGE AND ANGER, BRAWLING AND SLANDER, ALONG WITH EVERY OTHER FORM OF MALICE. BE KIND AND COMPASSIONATE TO ONE ANOTHER, FORGIVING EACH OTHER, JUST AS IN CHRIST GOD FORGAVE YOU."
> —EPHESIANS 4:31-32

How do you stand down from a state of siege? What do you do with unresolved anger? There is only one way to resolve the anger of past hurts. That way is forgiveness. God is serious about forgiveness, neither taking it lightly nor considering it optional.

When Jean realized she was acting like her mother, she was shocked. She'd sworn to herself, she wouldn't make the same mistakes; yet here she was following in her mother's footsteps. Repulsed, Jean grabbed up her distraught toddler, apologizing to her and hugging her close. When Emily reached up, patted her face, and gave her a sloppy kiss, Jean experienced the relief of forgiveness.

That day, which had started out so stressful, became a turning point for Jean. A small crack appeared in Jean's defensiveness against her mother. As Jean realized she was capable of the same hurtful attitudes as her own mother's, the crack widened, allowing forgiveness to establish a foothold in Jean's heart. In time, Jean stopped looking at her mother as the powerful force of her childhood and saw, instead, a broken and bitter woman. Forgiving her mother allowed Jean to win a decades-old battle and come to a sense of peace.

GRACE HAS BEEN DEFINED AS GOD'S UNMERITED FAVOR.

Forgiveness

Forgiveness is essential to living grace-full. Grace, in a Christian sense, has been defined as God's unmerited favor. Though we do not deserve it, we are forgiven because of Christ. In the same way, we are told to forgive others as God in Christ forgave us. God extends his grace to us, and he expects us to extend that grace to others.

When you live your life full of bitterness and unresolved anger, that life is full of stress. People must be constantly watched for the harm you know they will do. Events must be meticulously controlled to avoid the pain you are certain will come. Under siege, you become a raw nerve of reaction, stressed out and defensive. Peace is so far away, you can't even see a glimmer of it on the horizon.

The only path to peace is forgiveness—turning bitterness into kindness and resentment into compassion. By doing so, you claim victory over your enemies by refusing to participate in the war. By claiming victory, you establish your own peace.

As you seek peace with your enemies, don't forget to look in the mirror. Sometimes the person we have the hardest time forgiving is the one staring back at us.

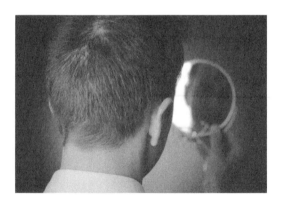

When you fail to forgive yourself, you may spend a great deal of time and energy attempting to make up for your faults, mistakes, and misjudgments. When you are at war with yourself, you're not going to experience peace.

In order to forgive—either others or ourselves— we need to learn to live gracefully. We must stop withholding forgiveness until certain conditions are met. We must stop demanding payment for forgiveness and offer it as a gift, just as God does.

I've heard more than one person tell me that forgiveness goes against their nature. Which nature? Children have an incredible capacity to forgive. Somewhere along the line, we can lose that capacity as adults, but that doesn't mean we never had it or can't get it back. Living grace-full means reconnecting with that capacity for forgiveness.

Risk

According to the calculus of this world, forgiveness— and the grace that it takes—doesn't add up. There are times when extending grace through forgiveness will be the exact opposite of what you feel like doing. Forgiveness seems risky and wrong.

Grace sets up its own internal contradiction because grace is not a human concept; grace is a divine concept. Author Phillip Yancey says, "Grace sounds a startling note of contradiction, of liberation, and every day I must pray anew for the ability to hear its message."[9]

No one said treating others with grace is going to be easy. Phillip Yancey says, "God took a great risk by announcing forgiveness in advance, and the scandal of grace involves a transfer of that risk to us."[10] Living grace-full means living risky and at peace with the risk. How can risk coexist with peace? When God is in charge of the equation, that's when. Don't stress about how all of this grace and forgiveness and risk and peace is going to work; trust God to figure it out for you. Ask him to show you the way to give grace and forgive; then follow where he leads.

> Ask him to show you the way to give grace and forgive; then follow where he leads.
>
> "MAY OUR LORD JESUS CHRIST HIMSELF AND GOD OUR FATHER, WHO LOVED US AND BY HIS GRACE GAVE US ETERNAL ENCOURAGEMENT AND GOOD HOPE, ENCOURAGE YOUR HEARTS AND STRENGTHEN YOU IN EVERY GOOD DEED AND WORD."
> —2 THESSALONIANS 2:16–17

STEP #6

Live Grateful

Susan walked in the door from work, looking forward to nothing more than putting her feet up and petting the dog. No sooner had she hung up her coat than her middle schooler entered the family room with a look of consternation and guilt on his face. *What now?* she thought, feeling her moment of tranquility evaporate. He was really sorry, but he'd forgotten about the science assignment that was due tomorrow and could she please help him get it ready?

Susan considered her alternatives. She could do like she'd done in the past and chastise him for his irresponsibility toward his schoolwork, his disregard for her, and his shortsightedness and lack of planning. With all of that ammunition, she could easily reduce his fragile sense of self to a smoldering heap of ash.

Should he have dealt with this sooner? Absolutely. But he was also a twelve-year-old trying to maneuver that awkward shift from grade school to middle school with multiple teachers and multiple homework assignments. Knowing the child that he was, she could also see a glimmer of the teen he was becoming. He was growing up so fast!

She was grateful he'd come to her with his problem, instead of hiding it. She was grateful he knew he could come to her for help. She was grateful she hadn't taken off her shoes, because her evening now included a trip to the store—maybe two.

"Let's see what you need," she said, holding out her hand. Relieved, he handed her the paper and together they went over the list. "I'm sorry," he told her in the car. "I know I should have done this sooner. I just forgot!" Susan was grateful for this teachable moment that could have turned out so differently.

■ ■ ■

The phone rang and Steve glanced down to see who was calling. Though he didn't really have the time to talk to his mother, Steve answered the call from her. The caregiver who was supposed to come and help with his father's care had called in sick—again—so could

Steve find a way to take them to the pharmacy to pick up their meds. What could he say? His parents were elderly, his father couldn't be alone by himself, and they needed their meds. Asking his mother to let him call her back, Steve took a breath and a minute to figure out how to make this work.

He had a meeting he needed to be at by seven, so if he left work on time and traffic cooperated, he could swing by their house, which wasn't far, and pick them both up. Then they'd head over to the pharmacy and he'd wait with his dad in the car while she went inside and picked up the meds. He could still drop them back at their house and make his meeting.

Calling her back, Steve let her know about the meeting but said he could be to the house by six fifteen. Delighted, his mother promised to have them both ready. She also said she'd make him a sandwich to eat in the car, so he wouldn't have to wait until after the meeting for dinner. His mother was like that, always thinking ahead. Steve was grateful for the sandwich. He was grateful he lived close by, so these kinds of trips were easier. He was grateful his mother was still able to care for his father in their home. He was grateful both his parents were still alive.

■ ■ ■

Nature hates a vacuum. As you leave behind stress and the negativity stress produces, you need to reach for positive thoughts, attitudes, and actions to fill in those empty spaces. If you don't, stress and negativity may come roaring back. As you fill yourself up with positive things, stress will have a harder time reestablishing a hold in your life.

Do you remember the story Jesus told about the impure spirit? I've found that Jesus' story has great application today when talking about de-stressing your life.

According to Jesus' story (found in Matthew 12:43-45), a man rids himself of an impure spirit. With this spirit gone from his life, the space it occupied remains empty. More than empty, the space is now swept, clean, and in order.

Roaming about, the impure spirit decides to go back to the man. Finding the space cleared out but unoccupied, the spirit sets up shop in the man, only this time he brings along seven others "more wicked than itself" (12:45). This man, Jesus said, is now worse off than before.

Jesus' story highlights the need not only to remove the negative but also to replace the negative with the positive. Empty spaces don't stay empty for very long. When you're de-stressing your life, it is not enough to get rid of the negative thoughts and emotions contributing to your stress; you must also replace them with positive thoughts and emotions.

> As you fill yourself up with positive things, stress will have a harder time reestablishing a hold in your life.
>
> "FINALLY, BROTHERS AND SISTERS, WHATEVER IS TRUE, WHATEVER IS NOBLE, WHATEVER IS RIGHT, WHATEVER IS PURE, WHATEVER IS LOVELY, WHATEVER IS ADMIRABLE—IF ANYTHING IS EXCELLENT OR PRAISEWORTHY—THINK ABOUT SUCH THINGS."
> —PHILIPPIANS 4:8

Attitude

One of the best positive attitudes you can stuff yourself with is *gratitude*. Gratitude is attitude and attitude is everything. Attitude determines how you choose to look at the world and what happens to you. Attitude determines how you respond to both the expected and the unexpected.

Being thankful for the pleasant is easy. Being thankful for the planned for, the known, the expected—pleasant or not-so-pleasant—is still relatively easy. Being thankful for the truly difficult, the challenging, and the painful is not easy at all. Yet what is the alternative? The difficult, the challenging, and the painful will happen. They are part of this life.

GRATITUDE IS ATTITUDE AND ATTITUDE IS EVERYTHING.

If we know these are part of this life, what should be our attitude toward them? Should we live in fear, stressed out and apprehensive about what is to come, on edge, defensive, and reactive, waiting for the other shoe to drop? How can you adopt an attitude of gratitude if you keep waiting for disaster? The answer is you can't. However, you can adopt an attitude of gratitude if you choose to look at the challenges of this life as avenues of God's blessing.

Much of the stress produced in our lives is due, not so much because of what we are doing, but because of how we *feel* about what we are doing. For example, when you are on vacation, doing fun activities and going new places, you may be busy from morning to night; but do you feel stressed about all of that activity? No! You are enjoying yourself, relaxing and being with friends and family, even though you are busy.

> You can adopt an attitude of gratitude if you choose to look at the challenges of this life as avenues of God's blessing.
>
> "CONSIDER IT PURE JOY, MY BROTHERS AND SISTERS, WHENEVER YOU FACE TRIALS OF MANY KINDS, BECAUSE YOU KNOW THAT THE TESTING OF YOUR FAITH PRODUCES PERSEVERANCE."
> —JAMES 1:2–3

So why is it that you can enjoy a busy vacation but become stressed over a normal workweek? Again, attitude is everything. When you are able to adopt an attitude of gratitude, resentment gets shoved aside, anger has no place to latch onto, fear finds no foothold.

Anger

Being stressed out and overwhelmed can leave you feeling powerless. When you feel powerless, you become susceptible to the siren song of anger. Anger makes you feel strong and empowered. Anger sustains you and fills your life with purpose and vindication for your pain.

Instead of gratitude, anger can crowd out despair and hopelessness. Anger can swell and press outward, providing a barricade against vulnerability. Anger can seem to be your protector, your vindicator, your savior. When that happens, anger becomes your god.

Powerful things have always competed with God for the devotion of people. In your stress, if you stand before the altar of anger, God says you can't stand in front of his altar:

> I tell you that anyone who is angry with a brother or sister will be subject to judgment. Again, anyone who says to a brother or sister, "Raca," is answerable to the court. And anyone who says, "You fool!" will be in danger of the fire of hell.
>
> Therefore, if you are offering your gift at the altar and there remember that your brother or sister has something against you, leave your

gift there in front of the altar. First go and be reconciled to them; then come and offer your gift (Matthew 5:22–24).

Rather than wanting us to be filled with anger, God wants us to be filled with gratitude. Anger drags us down while thanksgiving lifts us up. We could feel angry when troubles befall us, but instead, God wants us to be filled with thanksgiving, because he can turn those troubles into a resilient faith.

Fear

Anger puts emotions on overdrive, contributing to stress. Fear reactions can also contribute to stress. Fear of the unknown, fear of being hurt again, fear of failure, fear of pain—any fear can produce a stress reaction. "Fear can keep us bound so that we live less and less of life. The cost is the life that we did not live because of the fear."[11] So says Cloud and Townsend in *God Will Make a Way*. I would add that the cost is the life that we did not live because of the stress.

> Gratitude-based thinking places us on a stable position of thankfulness.
>
> "LET THE PEACE OF CHRIST RULE IN YOUR HEARTS. . . . AND BE THANKFUL."
> —COLOSSIANS 3:15

Gratitude is an antidote for fear. Fear focuses on all the things that could go wrong. Gratitude focuses on all the things that have gone right. When our gratitude is based upon the power and promises of God, we have an abundance of things that have gone right!

Fear-based thinking places us in a shaky position of insecurity. When our position is shaky, we become stressed, wondering not *if* we're going to fall but *when*. Disaster becomes a certainty.

Gratitude-based thinking places us on a stable position of thankfulness. We are able to identify the ways we are blessed and connect with the positives in our lives. Because we know we have been blessed, we *are* blessed, and we are able to anticipate being blessed even more.

Guilt

Guilt is an insidious reaction that contributes to stress. Guilt cries out, "Never enough!" When you feel guilty or ashamed or you blame yourself for not being or doing all you think you're supposed to be, you can never find peace. Relentlessly goaded by guilt, your life becomes a stress-filled attempt to make amends. Guilt is a crushing load that breaks the back of even the strong. No one can bear up under it. Few things rob us of peace and create stress in our lives more than guilt.

> As a Christian, I accept the reality of falling short.
>
> "FOR ALL HAVE SINNED AND FALL SHORT OF THE GLORY OF GOD."
> —ROMANS 3:23

We feel obliged to make room for our guilt; we pick it up and carry it around with us wherever we go. Guilt, therefore, is a prime candidate for sneaking its way back into our lives, if we don't replace it with gratitude.

Not all guilt is wrong, of course. Each of us has a conscience, an internal barometer of right and wrong. As a Christian, I accept the reality of falling short (Romans 3:23).

False guilt, however, has a way of appearing uninvited from unreliable sources, and it is often inappropriately transferred from the guilty to the innocent. I've found this in adults who had difficult childhoods. When they were children, the adults in their lives transferred to them their own guilt for neglect, substance abuse, verbal abuse, emotional abuse, rage, or lack of success.

LIVING GRATEFULLY MEANS LETTING GOD DETERMINE WHEN ENOUGH IS ENOUGH.

False guilt is especially stressful because there is no way to make amends. The truly guilty refuse to accept responsibility, no matter what you do. You cannot work hard enough, do enough, or be enough to remove the guilt, because the guilt was never truly yours in the first place. The stress you feel today may be from carrying around this false guilt from your past. Already loaded down, you're trying to carry around the added demands of your own life, and the weight is too much.

Gratitude is an antidote for guilt. When you feel guilty, you focus on what's missing and strive to make up for the loss. When you feel gratitude, you focus on what you have, not on what you don't. Guilt says, "This isn't enough;" but gratitude says, "This is enough." Living gratefully means accepting when enough is enough. Living gratefully means letting God determine when enough is enough.

When I was growing up, in church we sang a song about counting your blessings; we were told to name them one by one. As a child, I remember trying to do just that. Somewhere along the way to adulthood,

I forgot that simple approach to gratitude. When did you last stop and count your blessings? Start with the most basic: life itself; then move on to food, clothing, shelter. How are you blessed physically or through your relationships? Each of us is blessed in so many ways, day by day, that we too often fail to appreciate those gifts.

As a reminder of your blessings, take each day of the week and assign it a blessing to be thankful for:

- Monday—your life and health

- Tuesday—your food, clothing, and shelter

- Wednesday—your employment or financial provision

- Thursday—your family and friends

- Friday—your mind and intellectual understanding

- Saturday—your free will and capacity to make choices

- Sunday—your salvation

Stress will always seek to find a place in your life, trying to crowd out God's blessings, obscure God's power, and drown out God's promises. Stress will always look for ways to rob you of your joy, thus stealing away your moments and squandering your years.

The anger, fear, and guilt of this world can produce so much that is negative. But God is able to take those negatives and turn them into positives. When you truly believe that, when your attitude is positive, you will find you have so much to be thankful for! Gratitude will cease to be such a chore, something that you must emotionally muscle your way through. When you recognize the blessings you have, gratitude will well up inside you with such force, it will be impossible to stop!

GOD IS ABLE TO TAKE THOSE NEGATIVES AND TURN THEM INTO POSITIVES.

Notes

1. American Psychological Association, *Stress in America: Paying with Our Health* (February 4, 2015), 10. http://www.apa.org/news/press/releases/stress/2014/snapshot.aspx (accessed October 7, 2015).

2. Computed using numbers from the United States Census Bureau, *State and County Quick Facts*. http://quickfacts.census.gov/qfd/states/00000.html (accessed October 7, 2015).

3. Pew Research Center, *America's Changing Religious Landscape: Christians Decline Sharply as Share of Population; Unaffiliated and Other Faiths Continue to Grow* (May 12, 2015). http://www.pewforum.org/2015/05/12/americas-changing-religious-landscape (accessed October 10, 2015).

4. Tim Chen, *American Household Credit Card Statistics: 2015*. http://www.nerdwallet.com/blog/credit-card-data/average-credit-card-debt-household (accessed October 29, 2015).

5. Centers for Disease Control and Prevention, *FastStats: Exercise or Physical Activity*. http://www.cdc.gov/nchs/fastats/exercise.htm (accessed November 4, 2015).

6. Covert Bailey, *The Ultimate Fit or Fat: Get in Shape and Stay in Shape with America's Best-Loved and Most Effective Fitness Teacher/Covert Bailey* (Boston: Houghton Mifflin, 1999), 89.

7. Centers for Disease Control and Prevention, *Division of Nutrition, Physical Activity, and Obesity: How Much Physical Activity Do Adults Need?* http://www.cdc.gov/physicalactivity/basics/adults/index.htm (accessed November 4, 2015).

8. Gregory L. Jantz, *Losing Weight Permanently: Secrets of the 2% Who Succeed* (Wheaton, IL: Harold Shaw Publishers, 1996), 110, quoted in Gregory L. Jantz, *How to De-Stress Your Life* (1998; Grand Rapids, MI: Revell, Spire ed, 2008), 107.

9. Philip Yancey, *What's So Amazing About Grace* (Grand Rapids, MI: Zondervan, 1997), 71.

10. Ibid., 180.

11. Henry Cloud and John Townsend, *God Will Make a Way: What to Do When You Don't Know What to Do* (Nashville, TN: Thomas Nelson, 2006), 187.